Dropshipping

—

Successful without ifs and buts

John T. Wild

DEDICATION

Dedicated to my young family, my wife Kathrin and our son Valentin..

CONTENTS

ACKNOWLEDGMENTS

My thanks go to my family and the family of my wife, as well as all other relatives for the active support of my projects.

.

1 FOREWORD

Dear reader,

thank you for choosing this book. My work as a lecturer at the Technical University of Munich often shows me inadequate business start-ups, partly by students, partly by employees. As well educated as many may be, unfortunately some young entrepreneurs forget their common sense or the so-called gut feeling.
Additionally, badly or wrongly informed results in a ticking time bomb, which means the financial explosion after few months or years.

Dropshipping is a relatively new player in the bouquet of business models. One more reason to write another guidebook to inform as many as possible so that you face the matter with reason and foresight. There will be no general "no" for you in this book. You will get help and support based on clear examples. In addition, you will have access to an online service, which will then always have up-to-date information for you. How serious would it be to provide you with a comparison of suitable hosting providers here in the book if the book were two years old? That would not make much sense.

The basics, however, which this book is intended to serve, will continue to exist as long as dropshipping exists. Access to the Internet offer you get via the website: www.storeshop24.com

All the "ingredients" for a successful online business are waiting for you here. For example, ready-made online stores incl. domain for a quick start in your business field, themes and plugins in comparison, cost analyses for domains and hosting, as well as the service providers in comparison, i.e. from the dropshipper to the provider of automation systems, shipping accelerator, etc..

But now, enough of the foreword. I hope you enjoy reading the book.

2 WHAT IS DROPSHIPPING?

Dropshipping is a trading system that has reached the European Union from the USA in recent years. Colloquially, one could say that it represents a separation of real supplier and real marketer. In short, the wholesale works together with dropshippers. But why this business model and why this separation?

Well, in the age of internet commerce, the usual online stores are no longer easily noticeable and discoverable in their multitude. The competition, especially among smaller online retailers, forces them, as if in a vicious circle, to invest vast amounts of money in marketing and advertising in order to be noticed on the market at all.

A "global player" in this market for some years now are the platforms of "social media" - the list next to Facebook, Pinterest, Instagram etc. is getting longer and longer.

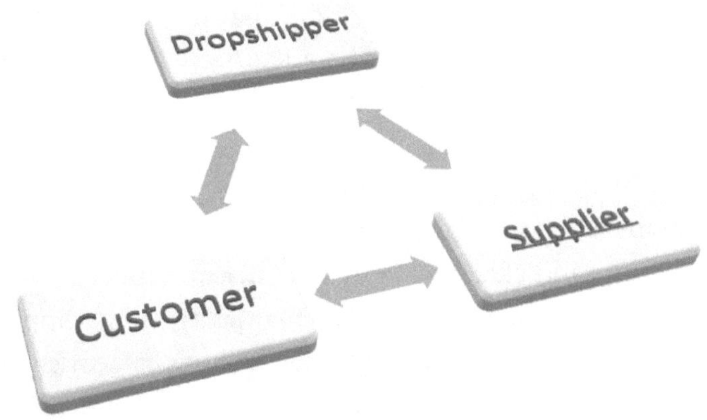

Now you might say: Okay, this is nothing new! But the Corona pandemic since 2020 has impressively shown us the market power that online retailing now has. The wave of digital procurement has reached even the last "analog consumer". In the lockdown, for example, one had to purchase vegetable boxes for the supply of fresh food in addition to masks, to name just   one   example.

The pandemic and online trading also had an impact on senior citizens. Even those who may not have had to deal with so many computers and the Internet at the time of their professional life now had to willy-nilly have a credit card and an e-mail inbox, learn to use a mouse and laptop, or keep seeking advice from their children and grandchildren. This group of buyers is well off and financially strong. As newly activated customers in the market, all the more so now. What's more, the following generations are already growing up online and take the Internet for granted. There will never be a shortage of customers here again in the future.

So why dropshipping? Dropshipping is also a form of rationalization, namely on the part of wholesalers. Skillfully and cleverly, the wholesaler no longer has to worry about advertising and marketing - he simply invites dropshippers. And this is how it works: a dropshipper creates a website and advertises a wholesaler's products there. The dropshipper makes sure that potential customers find his site. Then prospective customers make purchases on the dropshipper's site and, ideally, pay immediately using a standard payment system or credit card. The dropshipper passes the paid order to the wholesaler and pays him minus his margin, which he retains. The wholesaler ships the goods directly to the dropshipper's customer. That's it. So you literally "drop ship", so that's what the wholesaler takes care of now. And now I need a guidebook for that? There are market participants who, after reading the previous lines, would now open such a business without being aware of the consequences. You don't just go into a butcher's shop and cut up your own animal - butchering is a skilled profession.

Feel free to pick up some other guidebooks on dropshipping. How many of them say that they made mistakes in the beginning and would do it differently if they wanted to start again? Do you, dear reader, want to make those mistakes first too? I think not! Preparation is everything. Safety first. In business management, you move defensively and also calculate the "worst case" - the worst possible event or outcome of a business activity. This guidebook will introduce you to dropshipping with a great deal of certainty - whether you are trading as an individual, or even looking to set up a corporation. We illuminate the path of a secure foundation towards business success.

3 PRELIMINARY CONSIDERATIONS ON THE LEGAL FRAMEWORK

As with any financial venture, there are tax consequences to consider. In no case, and there is really no reason to do so, should you mess with the state tax authorities. In this age of the Internet and creeping data protection, the public authorities have far-reaching insights into payment flows. And by "messing with" they also mean not starting a business activity until a notification has gone to the tax office and your business registration has been filed with the relevant city or municipality. There is one fact that you do not have to report - that would be permanent losses. But this is not the aim of a successful business.

So if you want to start dropshipping as an individual, a business registration is sufficient at first. The trade office will register you with the tax office. From there you will receive a questionnaire for tax registration. The involvement of a tax advisor is not absolutely necessary, but in the interest of safety it is definitely an advantage. This can be seen from the extent to which the tax registration questionnaire asks for the assistance of a tax advisor. In the best case, you should not receive any payments before the date of business registration.

Playing it safe is especially important if you separate your business from your personal life. This way you can try your hand without endangering other family members or falling into worry. Unfortunately, this security costs knowledge and money. Not everyone wants to go down the path of setting up a corporation right away. And yet, it is possible and advisable. In the US you will have to fount a limited liability company (LLC).

With respect to the europien market, especially the german market, two options are practicable here: the UG and the GmbH. Now here are the hard numbers: For a GmbH, you would need € 25,000, of which you only have to pay € 12,500 into a business account. In the case of a GmbH, you are allowed to set up a so-called non-cash company - for example, you can bring in your private car. Of course only to the current market value, whereby a small appraisal would become due with the TÜV. Depending on the value of the used car, you then only need to pay a little extra to reach the minimum contribution of a GmbH. Advantage thereby: The car is already in the company and is written off immediately. The loss in value must now no longer be borne by you as a private individual, but by the state, since it will reduce your profit. Disadvantage: Now you have to pay tax on the private use and declare it in your tax return. Yes, but another advantage is that now all workshop invoices, TÜV costs and expenses for the insurance are in the company as expenses and no longer with you privately. You will think of these lines in this guide again when you are allowed to feel the effect of this construct.

The smaller possibility to establish is the so-called UG (limited liability). The addition in brackets may not be omitted and left out, because otherwise the limitation of liability is endangered, which was nevertheless goal. The UG can be created starting from one euro. If one considers the notary costs (yes, without notarial opening here unfortunately nothing goes) and the costs for the trade register entry, then € 400 to € 500 go out for this, which may be paid from the capital of the UG.

The time required to establish a corporation is about 4-6 months. If you read something different, be warned. Even a notary tells you at the appointment of notarization that the entry in the Commercial Register would take only 3-5 working days. What the notary does not tell you is that he will not forward the entry to the Commercial Register until he has been paid. Depending on the secretary's office, you may have to wait two weeks for the invoice. Then there is the bank transit time for the transfers, as well as the reaction latency of the authorities. After about a month you will receive the notification of the entry in the commercial register, which of course will be sent to the notary first, who will then forward it. Depending on the secretariat ... but I already said that. The current processing time for a VAT ID is three months, but this only starts to run when the trade office has forwarded your application.

However, for the business registration you need the notarial extract from the commercial register. If you register your business online, it will take another 4-5 weeks. If you co-inform the tax office with good intentions and already fill out and send in the questionnaire for tax registration, it can happen that you will not hear anything more about it, because at the same time there is no business registration yet. Then you will probably suddenly receive an analogous questionnaire sent to you again. Please fill it out again and send it in on time (tax offices have surprisingly short deadlines of one to two weeks).

Failure to respond to a letter from the tax office may also be construed negatively against you. If something is wrong or you cannot react in time, please arrange an extension of the deadline as soon as possible (in writing!). If you give good and truthful reasons, you will receive a 4-6 week extension.

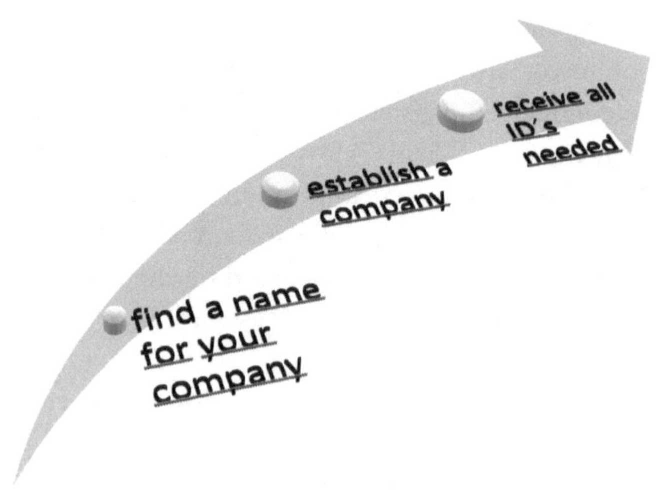

Checklist:

Example of founding a UG or GmbH in Germany (limited liability) in Germany

- IHK inquiry about the planned name of the UG
- research notary with experience in founding companies

- send the IHK confirmation to the notary in advance by e-mail
- make an appointment with the notary, lead time from one week   -   Hold notary appointment, sign deeds, get confirmation for bank

- Submit confirmation for the bank to a suitable commercial   bank

- Wait for bank account data to be received and transfer capital contribution as per notary's deed

- Send bank confirmation of company account with bank confirmation of receipt of payment to notary

-    Notary   sends   invoice   for   notarization

- Pay notary's invoice, Notary sends documents to local   court

-              Commercial   register   entry

-    Make   transparency   register   entry   yourself

- Local court sends invoice for commercial register entry

- Pay local court invoice and monitor entry online

- Local court sends confirmation of entry to notary

- Notary sends confirmation to you

- Business registration of corporation with confirmation from notary

- Tax office questionnaire for tax registration completed and sent in - Wait

4 WHERE DO YOU STATR YOUR DROPSHIPPING?

You couldn't really care less about the question from the chapter heading, could you? No, here already lurks the first trap in dropshipping, namely from the perspective of legal regulations - keyword "imprint". It crucially depends on which customers you address in your internet presence and on which place in the world the server is located on which your website is hosted! Is that important? Well, yes. If you are targeting German customers with hosting in Germany, the regulations in Germany apply. Proceed in the same way in Austria and Switzerland.

But what about the USA? There is no "imprint"

there. Some legal advisors even assume a discrepancy between both systems (i.e. EU to USA). So your path may lead you to already having to exclude customers of certain regions on your website, having to create multiple websites for different regions. The tip at this point is that dropshipping can and should grow. Don't go overboard right at the beginning. Decide to enter the market with a few products in a market that you know and therefore can estimate rather.

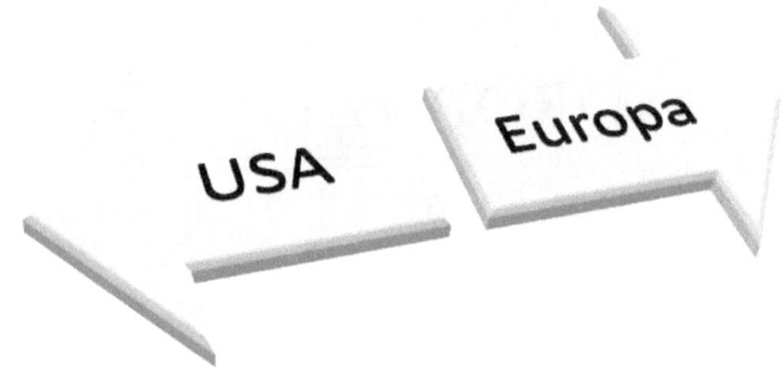

When looking for a suitable hosting, you cannot avoid contacting the provider by mail and asking for the location of their servers. If you do not receive a satisfactory answer, please look for another provider. Some providers understand the legal situation described here well and are prepared to answer your questions.

For the market entry in the USA you need two tax

advisors, because many applications you may submit in the states only with a representative, as long as you do not have a company headquarters and the appropriate tax registration there. You have to keep an eye on the follow-up costs and may protect against a too fast market expansion.

5 HOW MUCH CAPITAL DO YOU NEED FOR DROPSHIPPING?

The following approaches are two possible assumptions for a secure beginning. Here, you will get a first view of financial amount of the investment needed.

Assumption 1:

You have experience with website building, or even CMS systems. Then you can already start with $ 3000,-. If you have founded a corporation, you should mentally reserve $ 500 of it for the settlement. Depending on the trading platform, $ 300 to $ 500 per year can be due for hosting and services (payment systems). Ongoing costs are also fees for the business account and IHK contribution.

Assumption 2:

You have no experience - then you have to buy a ready-made store of a provider, suitably with products and contacts to the wholesale trade, which corresponds to your ideas. Serious providers on the Internet take for such a complete solution about € 2,000, - . You have to plan for this and start with more capital. With $ 5,000, - but it is certainly possible to get a functioning dropshipping store, and to bear the running expenses until sustainable income is   achieved.

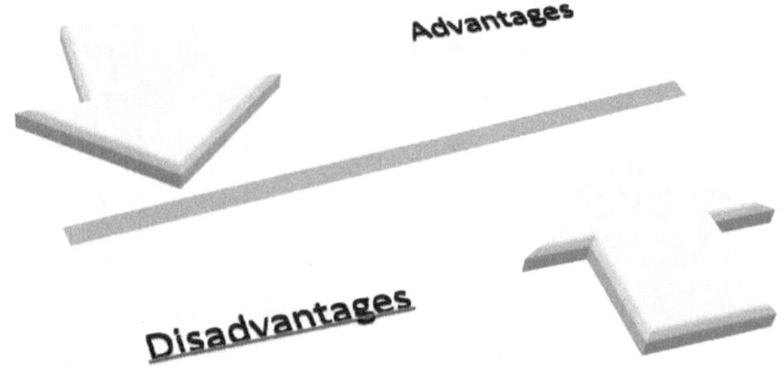

6 YOU WOULD LIKE TO TAKE OVER A RUNNING STORE?

Dropshipping is a business model that strongly depends on continuity, both in the offer and in advertising. There are several trading platforms where you can buy ready-made business branches, which have also been on the market for several years. Among them are many dropshipping businesses, which are offered at, in my view, totally exorbitant prices. I am afraid that many a supplier will come across an inexperienced customer and turn such a dropshipping store on him.

Why am I so negative here? Business models are being sold here that have only been on the market for a few weeks - at prices that are made up of several times the annual sales that can be calculated from them. And that for straight once an economic test balloon with tidy advertising budget, without writing in the sales text, how highly the expenditures for advertisement were for it. Or second trap here: Turnover is extrapolated on the basis of one month for the whole year. This is not the truth and the potential buyer will have to spend quite a bit of money on advertising to achieve this over the year. I have seen listings calling $70,000 for a dropshipping business with no inventory that has only been "tried out" online for 12 weeks. This is where the seller's eyes shine the most in the end.

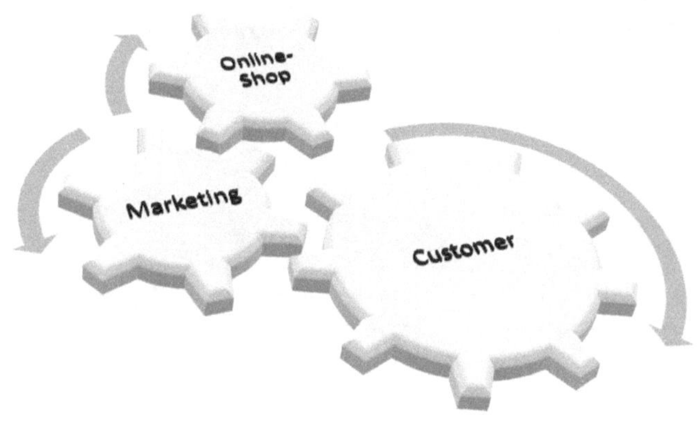

Considering the real expenses for a new creation of a website per year of $ 500 including hosting and operating the payment systems, there is no cheaper way to test the intended concept of your store than by doing it yourself.

On the site www.storeshop24.com you will find everything you need for this - whether it should be a ready-made store that allows you to get started immediately or an individual customization - we are especially happy to take care of "special cases".

The same applies to marketing. What you won't find in this short guide, you'll find on said website, including a think tank for a concise social media perception of your business. Another focus is on "unique content" - that is, search engine friendly and unique content for your website to optimize SEO ranking. Feel free to contact us.

7 WHICH PRODUCT SHOULD I DROPSHIP OR OFFER?

The right niche for their product range should be where you personally know well. You should not sell kitchen accessories if you do not like cooking and eating. You should not open a sports store if you are unathletic and so on.

There are some difficult products that you should generally avoid. From a responsible and legal point of view, these are, for example, food. After all, you as a seller are liable for quality here. Imagine if there were poisonings. Something like this will bring you and your dropshipping business to its knees to such an extent that insolvency may be imminent.

The same applies to cosmetics, prohibited goods in general or drugs. However, difficult products are also products with a high return rate. These are mainly clothing. Within the clothing then in particular still swimwear. Since you as a dropshipper usually have to bear the returns financially, special attention is paid to the products with the "does not fit problem". It is important that you do not start with such products either. With grown experience in dropshipping you may of course also offer difficult products.

Legally, you are only a seller and not a manufacturer, but in the case of difficult products, the first entry into the economic circle - in this case the EU - is what counts in terms of liability. This means that if you sell a product outside the EU, you suddenly become a manufacturer and therefore fully liable. Please consider now, you would not have founded a corporation and would operate dropshipping as a sole proprietorship - your whole family's existence may be exposed to financial ruin. That is why good prior planning is so irreplaceable in business. And by the way, no one has ever died from being overly cautious.

A quite safe niche is jewelry - preferably genuine and self-designed. Luxury items are always a constant, albeit with a longer start-up phase in which the young dropshipper's store must first be found.

8 WHICH WHOLESALE SUPPLIER IS THE RIGHT ONE FOR ME?

The suppliers, as the dropshipping suppliers are called, are widely spread around the world. Although the Chinese suppliers are the largest market players here, there are always quality problems. In addition to difficult delivery due to distance, language is often a barrier.

However, Asian suppliers in particular cultivate trade and personal discussions. In case of delayed or missing deliveries, you as a dropshipper have to explain to your customers. Valuable contacts can be quickly jeopardized. In addition, you have the market entry problem with the liability transferred to you when selling products in the EU.

There are supporting providers for a monthly fee that speed up the shipping of Chinese manufacturers to the USA, for example. However, even these companies cannot vouch for the supplier.

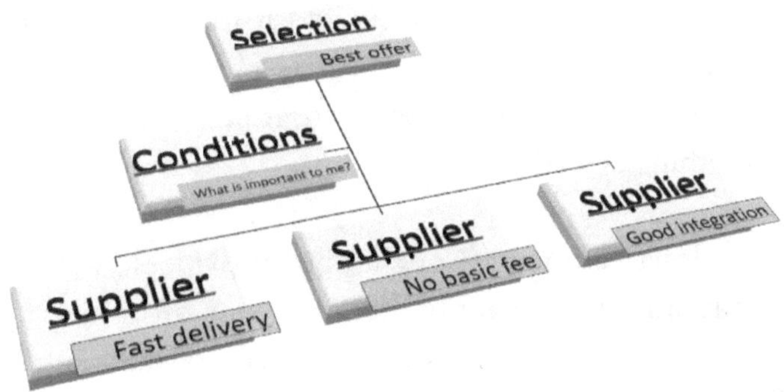

The issue of customs has not yet been addressed. That is certainly the bigger problem in the EU. Especially if the customer orders from an EU store and suddenly receives a package from China, on top of which he has to pay customs duties. What do you think? How does your customer feel then? Will he buy from you again? And what do you do with the returns? Shipping to China is not the same as shipping from China - feel free to test it. In this case, returns would go to you. But that's not what we wanted....

So here's an important fact: First, please choose your supplier based on returns management. And second, choose a supplier from the same market environment as your customers: So EU supplier for EU customers and USA supplier for USA customers for example.

The suppliers have completely different business models. It should be clear to every dropshipper that service costs. Some suppliers add it to the cost price for the dropshipper, while others charge a monthly fee in advance. And that's regardless of whether something is sold or not.

The least attractive might be providers with a minimum order quantity, because your dropshipping customers might not want to stick to that either. Dropshipping providers who charge a fee when they provide a service are advantageous. Personally, I think that's fair and prefer these market participants. Alternatively, there is also the one-time fee in advance. However, everything from insignificant to expensive is available here. If you want to find yourself in dropshipping first, you should not make any pre-commitment.

After all, the suppliers are also competing with each other for a good deal. If you have the idea to renegotiate the offers, then this will be granted with sales figures of 500 units per month. Below that, you will usually not get a personal contact. But here you can see what is possible in dropshipping. You can also use this to your advantage.

9 SHOPIFY OF WOOCOMMERCE?

Two classic representatives of two different persuasions are on the one hand "Shopify" as a platform provider of quickly set up stores and the OpenSource concept "WooCommerce", which is actually based on the WordPress system and becomes WooCommerce by means of plug-ins.

Shopify has a clear cost structure and offers quite a lot of service included in the price. For this, the fee also starts immediately, namely before you even want to click Start, or even convinced whether all systems are running properly. This means that you have to pay $29 to be online at all. In the basic configuration, there are unfortunately only a few themes at Shopify, so visual interfaces or even the layout structure. This now wants to be paid individually and also monthly. There are also offers with a one-time purchase price. In addition to a basic connection to social media, however, there are numerous other plug-ins, which often come with high costs.

One class of plug-ins will not be resisted in the long run - namely automation. In dropshipping, after all, you collect orders and pass them on to wholesalers. In the basic configuration of the store systems, Shopify like Woocommerce, this is all a lot of manual work. Even with only 10 orders a day, you have to schedule working time for this, order confirmations, shipping confirmations, codes for tracking the packages, processing payments.

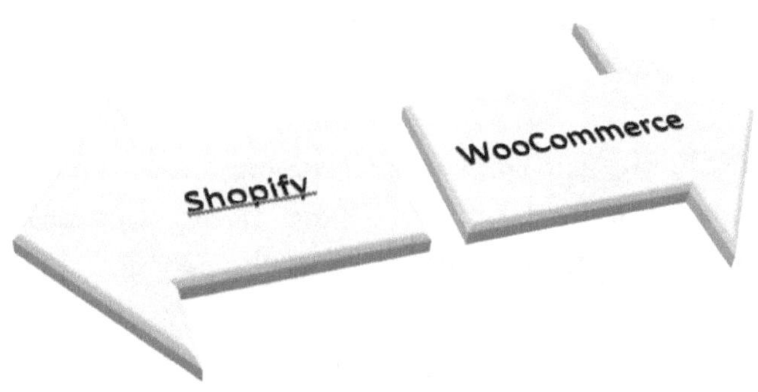

If you have started dropshipping after reading this guide, please make a log of your time spent. Many young entrepreneurs already get bogged down in calculating forgetting themselves and their own effort. Are you wondering if your margin is too small? Are you honest with yourself and measure your own work time correctly? I don't want to bully you, but it should be a pleasure for you to dropship besides the very clear financial aspect. But also think about your health and that you should be satisfied with the activities you spend time on.

In the next step, consider how much money you would have earned if you had worked the measured time in your previous or still existing job. For this sum (extrapolated per month), now please imagine that you would hire a second person to do this job (simple work, not particularly trained). Which is more profitable?

Using an automation plug-in, or doing the work yourself or having employees?

So Shopify and also WooCommerce mean a certain basic amount of fixed costs per month. Contrasting and evaluating both systems doesn't really do much at this point. You are quicker to market with Shopify, but you can replicate everything with WooCommerce and preserve your influence on the overall system.

Decide for yourself - Shopify lets you try it for free for 14 days. WooCommerce is OpenSource - some woocommerce hosting plans also offer a short free trial period.

10 YOUR GOLDEN MOMENT – THE BRILLIANT IDEA!

Is that moment coming for you, too? Oh yes, it will come. Perhaps quite unexpectedly and suddenly. Unexpectedly fast it will be and it will fill you with joy. Business ideas can be so wonderful - an adrenaline rush for the troubled vein. If enthusiasm came across, it was not unintentional. What it takes is plenty of research and, most importantly, time - your time. Because while you may have to wait for all the formalities of the state, you are certainly interested in the various business fields in dropshipping.

What is important in your considerations and thoughts is that you have time and do not put yourself under pressure. Therefore, a start-up and an entry into dropshipping from unemployment is not necessarily easy. However, if it is, please apply to the employment office for the appropriate subsidies to start your own business. It may not be much, but you cannot afford to do without money at this point. If you want to try it out and are still working in your existing employment it is just ideal to start dropshipping. Give yourself a time horizon and stick to it. You should also check how realistic your expectations of success are. If you start with dropshipping you also need a long breath. Quickly promised profits can be generated artificially by means of marketing, but advertising expenses will once again become your enemy along the way. What really counts is a continuously growing business. This also includes a not hasty start without haste and haste. Ask yourself the following questions and write your answers on an extra sheet of paper:

-        Where   do   I   know   best?

  - What are my hobbies?

- Am I creative?

- Can I talk well and convince people with it?

- What are my interests on the Internet?

- Which pages on the Internet does your wife visit? And with that we raise the first intensive questions:
 - What is my target group? Men or women?

- Which product would I like to sell?

- Do others also sell this product?

 - How many competitors are there in the market?

- At what price are the competitors offering? What could motivate the interest group to buy from me, when there are other offers on the Internet?

- I offer cheaper! Can you really do that? Do you then still have a profit?

- I combine products new as a set! Yes, this can work.
- My product is better because... - more durable - more functions - - easier to disassemble - - easier to recycle - - higher load capacity - - fail-safe - - etc.

You can see from this what questions need to be

asked. And by you. Honestly and truly. Without ifs and buts. You should avoid products for which you can only answer these questions inadequately.

11 TRAFFIC – AND THE PROBLEM WITH TRAFFIC

Many city centers have major problems with vacancies. On the one hand, more and more discounters and outlets are moving to greenfield sites, while on the other hand, municipalities are happy to react with parking fees against tight budgets that the traffic calming of the city center may have cost them. A small side blow for all those who are still wondering about this. On top of that, rents in downtown areas are no longer a bargain.

So more and more business models can no longer function. Those that are still there have smart customers who Google the store price while still in the store online and, of course, find cheaper offers on the Internet. Outraged by the high price in the store, the customers go and now order the identical product online.

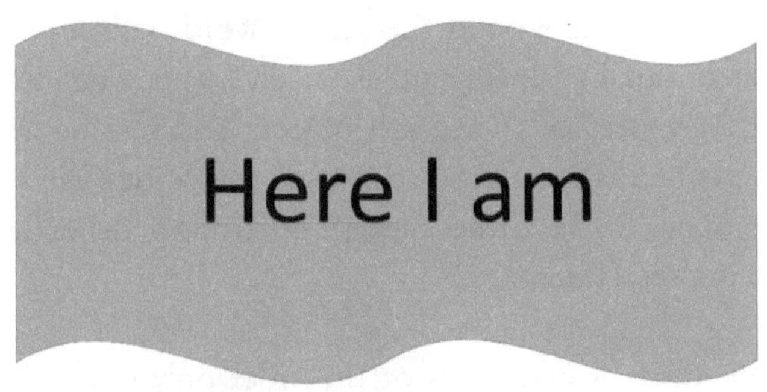

You don't want that to happen to your new dropshipping store. The customers should become more and not less. With your decision to learn about dropshipping, you have certainly taken a step in the right direction. Online retailing is the future. However, you need to actively take care of "getting found" on the Internet. This is a weak point of many slow-starting stores in dropshipping. A real wave of customers is needed, however, because only customers who come looking can also buy.

The basic step is, as always, optimization for the search engine (SEO optimization). Here you can find numerous instructions on the Internet. Good and fast it goes via video on the most popular platform. The effect of this measure is from rather long-term. Fast sales this does not generate.

A second step can be the switching of announcements in the search machine. Here you offer however around the search word with a price, which can be already quite stately depending upon attractiveness of the search object. And just because someone clicks on your ad doesn't mean they will buy anything. So here the success is strongly dependent on the search term.

Sometimes it even pays off to order only one aspect of the product as a search term, which may have been forgotten by other providers. But things only really get going with the social media channels. And fast above all.

There are numerous lists of influencers circulating on the Internet to whom you can gladly make an offer for a post about your product. You will certainly get these euros back several times over. The prerequisite is the right product with the right influencer and the right target group. And here lies the rabbit's foot again. Here you need to gain experience and not put all your eggs in one Influencer's basket. Once a successful collaboration has been found, it should be secured.

12 ADVERTISING AND BUDGET

Difficult question, difficult answer. Of course, it depends on the product and the target group. If you want to do a test that gives you an initial indication of your assessment, you should spend $ 500 in the first month. That is then a small campaign. But please also then only when you can deliver products as dropshippers in sufficiently large numbers.

Please do not do this with one product. Here should be 5-10 products already at least in the offer. Your advertising should be quantitatively constant. It will also not do you much good to be represented on really every platform of the social media. Observe your customers. Which platform comes into question then? Or where do you have the most search engine hits on your topic area in social media? The topic of advertising and marketing is constantly changing and will certainly fill another book about it.

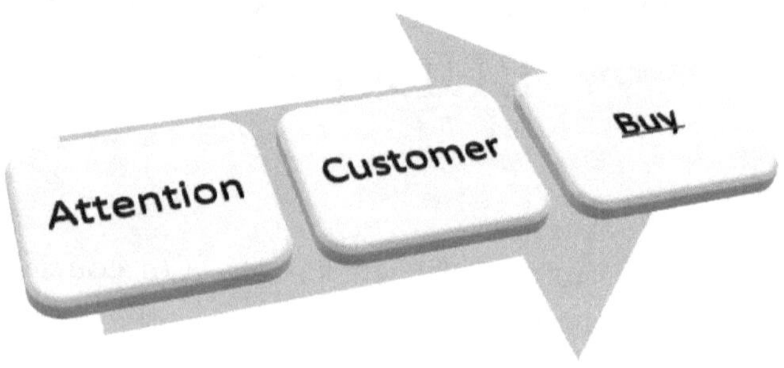

13 PROMISES OF PROFIT AND REALITY

You know the promises of dropshipping guides? Of course, positive advice sells better than constant doom and gloom. But a realistic reality must be allowed - and "without ifs and buts" seriously enlightens you at this point. The sums titled as "profits" are usually only the turnover figures, i.e. here of course still the payments to the supplier go off. Then, of course, you have to pay the payment system, usually a single-digit percentage of sales (!!!), not just from your margin. Depending on the store system, you still have to list the expenses and think of the expenses for advertising. Do you check yourself? Do the other market companions in the advice landscape always show how much turnover is opposed to which advertising budget? Probably not! Let's assume you have a dropshipping margin of 10% (and I think 10% is well within reach, you shouldn't start dropshipping below that), then let's imagine that your dropshipping store turned over € 100,000 last year. Of this 80% goes as costs to the supplier, 5% as expenses for losses from returns, 3% for the payment system and 2% for hosting the platform and plug-in costs. So in this example you are left with € 10,000.

But is that already your profit? If we consider only the taxes on the part of the tax office and additionally consider trade tax, we can calculate with half of the amount as business result. It is now further no other source of income, so we divide the remaining € 5,000, - by twelve, in order to come on a monthly result. Now we have monthly about € 417, -.

If you are the managing director of a corporation, your personal tax rate would still be deducted if you distribute completely and only to yourself. An annual turnover of € 100.000,- and at the end a salary that is not even on the level of the basic income support in Germany? And further: How many hours did you have to work per month for that? Please be honest... Do you still reach the minimum wage?

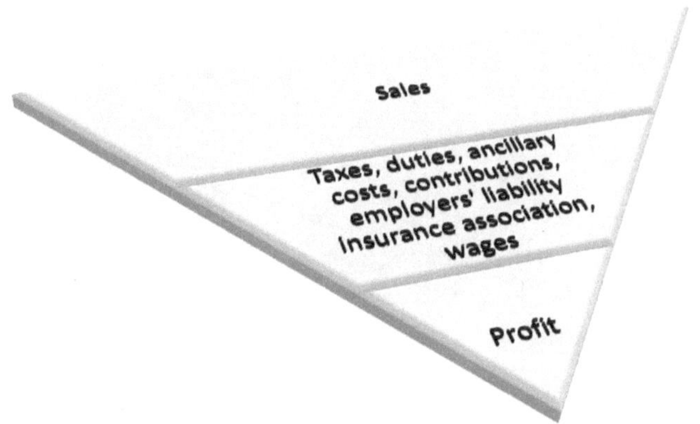

And now a realistic view of dropshipping pays off. No ifs, ands, or buts. Don't get me wrong, I'm not trying to dissuade you, but many fast or gullible founders start out this way and eventually realize something is wrong. So to truly succeed in dropshipping, we need to rethink - not like so many others before you.

To break the central example of this chapter and put the overall concept of dropshipping on a good and economic footing, we need to change one or more set screws in the system. These can be:

- Find better suppliers, lower cost prices

-Individualization: Own design
-Brand building: Individualization through your own "name"

-Reduce working time: Automation as a solution   - Increase sales: Scale your business to 2030:

14 THE RIGHT SUPPLIER AND CORRECT ONBORDING

The major dropshipping suppliers are reliable partners. Having them on board is certainly not a mistake. Unfortunately, the margins to be achieved are rather low and the products are also available from any other supplier.

On top of that, there is often a monthly flat rate regardless of orders and sales. You should not enter into this. The research is lengthy. You will find numerous suppliers on the Internet who would be happy to do this work for you, for money of course. These companies and the big suppliers dominate the first pages of your search engine with great reliability. So keep on browsing. From search engine page five on, it gets interesting. Please look around also in the neighboring foreign country, if you have linguistic advantages.

There you will sometimes still find companies that are just starting with dropshipping offers and are therefore happy to enter new sales channels.

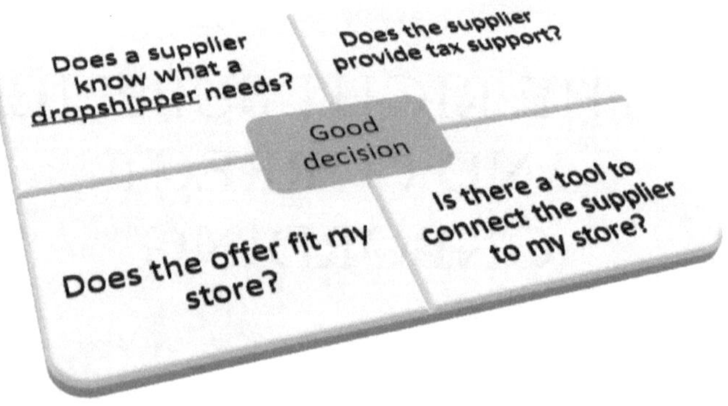

Politely introduce yourself as an entrepreneurial person and describe your business plan. If you get open answers, then you are on the right track. If, on the other hand, you are handed a cost table that you are supposed to enter into before they even talk about specific products, you should continue your Internet research. Often it is simply a gut decision, because in the long run both sides have to feel comfortable. You can find a current comparison of major dropshipping providers at www.storeshop24.com.

15 INDIVIDUALIZATION – YOUR OWN DESIGN

The next option for increasing margins is to design your own product. To do this, you need to look for so-called "white label" manufacturers or suppliers. At first, this is not as difficult as you might think. You can even get nutritional supplements mixed according to your wishes and recipes as a white label. With such a supplier, you only need the logo and design of the packaging and off you go with your "own" product. Partly only pallets are delivered, partly the minimum order quantity is 1 - so it is also suitable for dropshipping, although often with the disadvantage of not being able to specify a packaging type. Branding is easy with additional flyers that you enclose with your commissioned shipments, small free gifts or simply the individual invoice. Here, too, there are differences - sometimes you have to supply elements, sometimes the supplier also takes care of printing the enclosures.

With a so-called "private label license" you reach the highest level of customization and permitted changes in the design. Here you are even allowed to make technical changes and call yourself the manufacturer.

16 BRAND BUILDING: INDIVIDAUALIZATION THROUGH YOUR OWN "NAME"

Before you can successfully establish a trademark, you must first ensure that you can also use the trademark securely and in the long term. For this, an application as a word mark or word/figurative mark at the patent office is indispensable.

From $ 300,- you are in. In return, you will have the trademark rights to the selected word for the next 10 years from the date of application for the trademark. In 10 years, however, you will have to pay much more for the renewal. Either you don't care by then and don't renew, or the trademark is so well established that renewal will certainly pay off for you.

Here is the checklist for trademark registration:

- Search in the database of the Patent Office, the DPMA, then EPO, then USPTO - so first Germany, then Europe and then USA.

- Search the Internet to find the same words or similar mentions - Tip: Do not name your trademark after a historically insolvent company - such things can be found on the Internet nowadays, unfortunately, for a very long time.

- Avoid clashing even slightly with products of large market players - they can certainly afford the warning procedure and will do so.

- Apply for your own trademark and pay the fee - wait, the current waiting times are given as 8 months, but express processing costs a significant surcharge - register the trademark in your name

- as soon as trademark is registered in Germany, you are allowed to do this in the EU and the USA as well - for this purpose, currently a document must still be filled out analogously.

However, the process is only possible from the moment of registration in Germany. - Second option:

Patent attorney. Patent attorneys do not cost very little, but they bring about a legally secure state quickly and safely. Permitted would be here also the direct way over the USA, since a representative is needed for the registration. Conclusion for trademark registration: Make sure that the e-mail accounts belong to you in the long run and that nobody can tamper with the names you have chosen.

It is not uncommon for large competitors to beat smaller players to the punch when they start business and attempt a trademark application. If this happens faster than you, in 8 months you will receive confirmation from the patent office that your application has been rejected. So you see: time is money and as soon as you achieve secure sales, the trademark application should have priority.

17 REDUCING WORKING TIME – AUTOMATION AS A SOLUTION

Both Shopify and WooCommerce provide automation solutions for your store. Shopify already internally from the higher performance levels above "Basic", WooCommerce exclusively via plug-ins.

The selection for both platforms is almost endless, of which really good and usable plug-ins can be paid their service safely in the monthly. My assessment here is that good performance must also be paid for - so functioning plug-ins also cost something. What should a good plug-in be able to do: - Check an incoming order for plausibility

- Cancel obviously incorrect orders

- Monitor receipt of money for the order

- Send e-mail to the customer with order confirmation - Forward correct orders directly to the supplier
- Pay the forwarded orders automatically

- Forward a sending code of the transport company to the customer via python script

- Monitor and report the delivery.

- Notify customers by e-mail.

Otherwise, you usually have to do each step manually. Companies have several employees for these processes. You have a plus point if you rely on reliable products - products that generate few returns. Another fact that makes the use of Chinese dropshipping providers superior. Often, however, your only option is to transfer data via CSV files. CSV is an old and common file format, which enjoys great popularity again. It connects your supplier with your store system in a simple way. You need a product CSV and an inventory CSV. The latter should be updated daily. The rabbit's foot in this matter is that in most cases synchronization is lacking. That which a plug-in accomplishes can make a lot of work for you by hand. The sorting of columns on each side of the data stream is individual, which means that you actually need a separate plug-in for each. And so, while many suppliers will tell you what the data stream looks like, you'll probably need a programmer after all. Phew - expenses again. Of course, there are also providers of suitable plug-ins for individual suppliers. But that has to be paid for in a monthly or yearly lump sum. Regardless of how much you dropship. The sums called are often in the range, for which money you would also get a completely built and connected store. The tip from me: Don't start a business, an online store and don't spend money until you have seen a working complete system with data connection. With providers with a free trial period this is possible. Partly for 14 days, partly for 30 days. In the USA partly only 7 days. It is worth a lot if later, when your business is running well, you have to take care of your store only a little intensive. Imagine you generate a nice passive side income with a store and want to expand your business to ensure your financial independence. Then you might need three online stores at the same time. At the latest then it shows who has paid good attention during the first steps, or who then has their head overflowing with work.

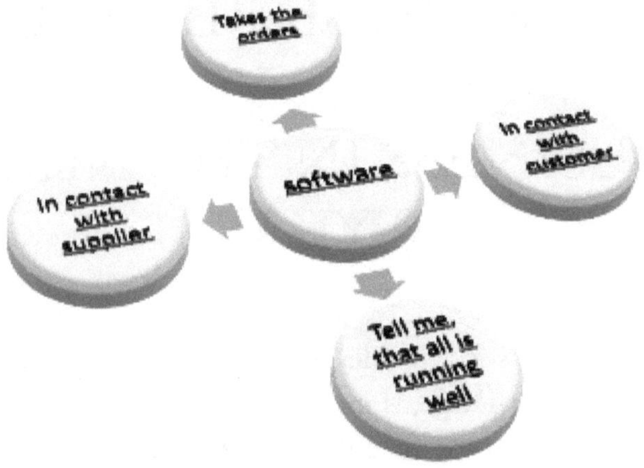
Takes the orders
In contact with customer
In contact with supplier
software
Tell me, that all is running well

18 INCREASE REVENUE – SCALE YOUR BUSINESS IN THE NEXT 10 YEARS

In times of social media, scaling, i.e. making initially smaller stores large, is no longer a real problem. First, there are plug-ins to choose from again, or a direct connection in the backend of your store. Nevertheless, social media will face a big problem in the next few years: Am I even visible with my company to my target group? Since online marketing and a booming market for the coming years, visibility is probably not always guaranteed. And in the future, it may not be the technology that still hinders you in marketing, but perhaps the idea behind your marketing to also create impact accordingly.

Of course, you hire an influencer and he will certainly do a good job, but in order to generate organic, i.e. real - real, traffic in the long term and to attract prospects to your own product, a continuous line and concept creation and adherence to it is needed. Again, feel free to get inspired by www.storeshop24.com.

19 THE MARKET ENTRY IN THE EU AND THE THING WITH THE TAXES

The lucrative market of the USA offers great advantages with regard to dropshipping. Advantages that probably have to be taken into account. First of all, there is the huge and especially same-speaking population group, which has a generally high sales potential, and secondly, there are tax advantages.

For trading in the EU you need a VAT number, registration even if you will not have a real location in the EU and registration with a local tax authority of an EU member state. You do not need a representative. The tax information refers to the customer according to the respective recipient country with its different tax rates. On websites, the costomers are familiar to get price inclusiv taxes and shipping, so you need to now the location of a potential customer to the beginning of shop-visiting.

Back to the Sitituation in the USA. What has been simply outlined in a few words is in reality highly complex and can finally only be done by a tax consultant with USA expertise or EU expertise. Not only does every state in the USA have a different sales tax regulation, even individual cities can levy a different amount of sales tax. As a dropshipper there are only two good ways to be in the USA, either with your own company 100% in the USA, or 0% in the USA.

All other states in the USA either do not have a sales tax, or make their tax liability dependent on economic nexus. This nexus arises only from $ 100,000 to $ 200,000 and in addition partly with the number of sales in a year for each individual state. Here the limits are often 100-200 sales made. Per year, mind you. The previous economic year applies to the assessment limit. Some states deviate again and consider only one quarter. By the way, the amount of sales does not matter. In states like New York, you quickly hit the limit, while other states would still run within the limits   for   a   long   time. So the rule is: In those states in the U.S. where your supplier has a warehouse or administrative office, you must promptly report to the IRS. A good place to start for addresses is the corresponding post on

Shopify. You will have no choice as a business owner outside the US but to fill out a form by mail. Exception would be you have a social security number in the US.

Whether you will be liable to pay tax in which state, and if so, in what amount, is something you and even the authorities have no way of knowing. The risk is that you do not file a tax and afterwards you have to pay taxes out of your margin. Here again, up to 7% can be lost quickly, depending on the sales tax rate in the state in question. Shopify offers a solution for many problems - that has to be conceded. For example, the store system reacts immediately as soon as you create a location in the USA as a shipping location. In the following step, you will be offered to register for tax payment via a partner - this friendly help costs $225 per state in the USA.

There are also cases where your targeted supplier answers "... there and there in the USA ..." when asked about shipping centers. This can only make you miss the mark as a dropshipper and put you in a bad position vis-à-vis the American tax authorities. A very bad idea. You can write off this supplier.

Have you ever thought about founding a company in the USA? Today it is quite possible to do this from home - but you still need a local law firm to handle it.

Anyway, you are in for € 3.600,- plus annual expenses of at least € 1.200,-. This includes postal address as well as financial administration. Three to four favorable states in the USA can be found out quickly on the Internet on the basis of my description. A big advantage, if this would come into question for you at all, would be the later possibility to emigrate to the USA. For this purpose the formation as a corporation is necessary. You can see how dropshipping could pay off for you.

20 THE LEGALLY COMPLIANT WEBSITE FOR YOUR DROPSHIPPING

... and that is not so easy. First of all, there is a constant legal change that you have to control constantly. One big problem is usually image rights. This is where "the big accidents" happen regularly in the "warning world". To give you an example - if you use five (paid or free) images without a source, for example, and you are warned off, you can face sums of $ 15

,000. These are circumstances that can get even a young GmbH into serious trouble. So please exercise the greatest care here.

In addition to the usual imprint (see EU requirements), the GDPR declaration on websites is important today. Each data processing and data collection point, search engines, as well as plug-ins

65

used, must be listed individually and the type of data collection described with scope and purpose. Advice on free tools and support is available at www.storeshop24.com.

21 A WORD IN CONCLUSION

Now you may have more questions than answers? Hm... that is actually the best starting position. Maybe you approach first with this small book, then inform yourself further on the website to the book and come so step by step to your successful business model according to the dropshipping principle.

Of course, other questions are important. You are welcome to be a guest of the Internet offer and study the contributions. They are always more up-to-date than the book can ever be. The fast running internet time with your constantly changing offers demands an equally fast adapting offer. Therefore my offer to you with the combination of book and website.

Please don't rush it - take it slowly. The steady drop wears away the stone. And should dropshipping not become your playground for achieving a passive income in the end, you have found this to be an independent decision for you this way.

After all, that doesn't mean you don't want to and can't make money on the Internet in another way. Stay up to date and well informed - then new opportunities will always arise for you, which you can integrate into your considerations.

Notes

Notes

Disclaimer:

The information provided in this book on economic procedures can mean the total loss of your capital if followed improperly, despite careful examination. Neither the author nor the publisher nor Wietratec UG (haftungsbeschränkt) are liable for any damages and losses caused by reading this book. No warranty or guarantee can be given for the completeness, correctness and topicality. The book serves the purpose of entertainment and reflects the experiences and opinions of the author. The contents of this book are not legal or financial advice. A guarantee for success or the achievement of individual goals described in this book is also not given. This book contains links to other websites in the e-book, as well as in the print version. The respective operator is responsible for the content of the linked pages. as well as for the legal admissibility. Illegal content has not been linked to the best of our knowledge and belief.

Imprint